NORTH CAROLINA
HOME
APPRAISALS

A Step-by-Step Guide for Buyers,
Sellers, and Real Estate Agents

North Carolina Home Appraisals: A Step-by-Step Guide for
Buyers, Sellers, and Real Estate Agents

ISBN 9798302748805
© Copyright 2024 by A. Jay Cottle

INTRODUCTION

Dear Reader,

I wrote the "North Carolina Home Appraisals: A Step-by-Step Guide" with a heartfelt desire to give back to our community and make the home appraisal process clearer and more accessible for everyone involved. Having spent over a decade as a real estate appraiser, I saw firsthand how crucial it is for real estate buyers and sellers to be well-informed. My goal is to empower you with the knowledge you need to navigate property appraisals with confidence, ensuring you can make informed decisions every step of the way.

Additionally, I wanted to provide real estate agents with a comprehensive guide to help them better serve their clients throughout the appraisal process. By sharing my expertise in this book, I hope to contribute to a more transparent and informed real estate market, ultimately benefiting our entire community.

Warm regards,

Jay Cottle III

TABLE OF CONTENTS

CHAPTER 1:

Introduction to Real Estate Appraisals

MYTH	**REALITY**
Home appraisers determine the property's market value.	Home appraisers estimate a property's value based on market data, but the market (buyers and sellers) ultimately determines the value.

What is a Real Estate Appraisal?

A Real Estate Appraisal is a third-party unbiased opinion of the fair market value of "real property." It's crucial for informed buying, selling, or financing decisions, ensuring fair pricing and loan security.

When and Why You Need a Home Appraisal

Getting a Primary / Secondary Mortgage: Lenders require an appraisal to ensure the property's value covers the loan amount.

Refinancing or HELOC: An appraisal determines current home value for a cash-out refinance or home equity line of credit. In a HELOC, you're borrowing money against the equity (market value-debt), at an interest rate that should be lower than a credit card. Your home becomes collateral for the loan.

Estate Planning or Divorce: Attorneys use the appraisal to establish property values at the date of death or separation, and then to divide real estate assets.

Selling Your Home Yourself (FSBO): Helps set the most probable sales price for your home.

Cash Purchase: An appraisal can ensure you're paying a fair price for a property.

What is Considered Real Property?

- **Real Property:** Anything permanently attached to the land. Example: a built-in refrigerator is real property if attached to the walls or cabinets.

- **Personal Property:** Items that can be easily removed without special tools, like a standard refrigerator.

- **Gray Areas:** Items like sheds, satellite dishes, microwaves, and security systems should be specified in the contract to clarify if they're included in the sale.

Types of Residential Real Estate

Single-Family Homes (SFR): A home on its own parcel of land, built on-site according to state building codes.

Townhomes: Homes that share a common wall with neighbors. Owners typically own the land beneath and the exterior of the unit.

Condominiums (Condos): Owners only own the interior of the unit (paint to paint), while common areas and land are managed by an HOA.

Modular Homes: Factory-built homes transported and assembled on-site, following state building codes. Be sure to keep the validation stamp, typically located on the inside of a cabinet door, which will be required for resale or refinancing.

 Manufactured Homes: Single family, built to a different code known as HUD standards, these homes have compliance certificates inside, typically on the inside of a cabinet door, and metal tags on an exterior corner. Do not destroy or remove these as they are both essential for resale or refinance.

 Raw Land: Undeveloped land with no infrastructure (water, sewer, power, utilities).

 Buildable Sites: Developed land with utilities ready for construction.

Appraisal Comparisons

Always compare similar properties: SFR to SFR, townhome to townhome, condo to condo. No mixing apples and oranges here!

CHAPTER 2:

The Home Appraisal Process

<table>
<tr>
<td>

 MYTH

All home appraisals are the same.

</td>
<td>

 **REALITY**

The real estate appraiser matters. While the process is standardized, home appraisers may have different approaches, expertise, different scopes of work, and access to credible data, leading to varying valuations.

</td>
</tr>
</table>

Hiring a Real Estate Appraiser

For primary/secondary mortgages, and HELOC loans, typically the lender will hire the appraiser. For estate planning, divorce settlements, for sale by owner, and cash buyers, the owner or buyer of the property will hire the appraiser. Be sure the home appraiser knows who the client is in relation to the property, specifically ask what type of appraisal you need, and what the purpose of the report is. Get a quote for the work and an estimated turnaround time in writing.

Types of Home Appraisals: InPerson vs. Desktop

In-person full interior/exterior inspection: (URAR 1004 UAD version form for lenders or general purpose form for others). The appraiser will inspect the exterior and interior of the home.

Exterior only, drive-by report: (2055 form for lenders). Exterior inspection only from the street. No contact with the homeowner shall be made. Real estate appraisers use tax records, MLS, and other third-party sources for data on the home/property. Exterior-only appraisals are less expensive, but can also be less accurate. The appraiser is assuming the interior condition.

Desktop/bifurcated/hybrid report: A third party inspects the property and a separate party completes the appraisal from their desk. This will speed the loan process, however, there are no regulations on who can inspect the property which could diminish the credibility and accuracy of a report. Only the licensed real estate appraiser is allowed to complete the report.

Steps in the Home Appraisal Process

Collecting Data: The appraiser collects data on the property including tax records, deed (ownership), real estate taxes, plat maps, surveys, and any other data to prepare for inspection and report development.

Inspecting the Outside: The appraiser will first inspect any external influences on the property and note the surroundings that could negatively or positively influence the value of the property. Some negative external influences include a busy road, corner lot, poorly maintained road, nearby railroad, surrounding properties such as a factory or other manufacturing facilities, airports, power lines, smells produced by farms/livestock, and any other unsatisfactory conditions for living.

Some positive external influences could include privacy setting, water views, golf course views, mountain, or other positive views, proximity to recreational activities (beaches, restaurants, entertainment, etc.).

The appraiser will measure the dwelling and any other improvements such as detached sheds, detached garages, and accessory dwelling units. The appraiser will note other permanent structures on the property including in-ground pool, fences, etc. The appraiser will make note of the quality and building material of the dwelling including exterior finishes (brick, Hardie plank siding, wood, and vinyl are some common exterior siding), type of roof (composite shingle, metal, cedar shake, terra cotta are few examples), the foundation of the subject (crawl, slab on grade, raised slab, pilings are common types), gutters/downspouts, window type, heating/cooling type, car storage (garage, carport), and driveway type.

Interior Inspection: The appraiser will measure and separate each component of the dwelling including heated square footage, garage sq. ft., porches, patios, sunroom, screen porches, decks, balconies, etc. The square footage is measured according to ANSI standards (American National Standards Institute) which has special requirements and standards for measuring the dwelling. The heated square footage must contain a permanent heat source and must meet certain height requirements. The minimum interior ceiling height requirement must be 7'. In areas with sloped ceilings, like a bonus room, the appraiser cannot include the area under the 5' height mark. These are just a few of the requirements, there are others.

The appraiser will sketch the dwelling and note the functionality (floor plan). Living room, kitchen, dining, bedrooms, baths, bonus rooms, office/study, den, sitting, etc. The appraiser will note if the floor plan contains any functionality problems and/or if the floor plan is common/typical for the market. If there are functional problems with the floor plan then the appraiser is required to draw this in the sketch and note them in the report.

Other items that the appraiser will note on interior inspection are condition, quality, floor covering, wall covering, trim/finish, bath floor covering and wainscoting, type of attic, and appliances. The appraiser should note any renovations, updates, or any other major work completed on the dwelling.

What's in the Report?

After collecting data and making the inspection, the appraiser will develop the report. The report consists of:

- ✔ Cover page
- ✔ Subject section
- ✔ Contract section (for purchases)
- ✔ Neighborhood section
- ✔ Site section
- ✔ Improvements section
- ✔ Sales Comparison Approach
- ✔ Cost approach
- ✔ Income approach
- ✔ Final Reconciliation of Value
- ✔ Project information for PUDs
- ✔ Addendums

- ✔ Building sketch
- ✔ Subject photos
- ✔ Property information (tax card, deed, etc.)
- ✔ Aerial map
- ✔ Flood map
- ✔ Survey
- ✔ Boundary map
- ✔ Comparable sales photos
- ✔ Market conditions report and/or any other supporting documents for a credible report

Delivery of report

A real estate appraiser can submit a report ONLY to the client via secure email, portal, physical copy, or other way where only the client can read it. The appraiser, according to Board law, is not allowed to deliver a home appraisal report to anyone other than the client. If a lender engages an appraiser to perform a property appraisal, then the appraiser can only send the report to the lender and not the homeowner or real estate agent.

CHAPTER 3:

What Factors Influence Home Value?

<table>
<tr>
<td>

 MYTH

Price per square foot is king and the only formula that matters.

</td>
<td>

 REALITY

Appraisers use many different tools and methods to determine appraisal value.

</td>
</tr>
</table>

It's the biggest myth in residential real estate appraisals! Many people mistakenly think price per square foot and comps are the driving factors of an appraisal. Truth is, there are many more considerations. Let's get into them!

Market Analysis vs Appraisal

A market analysis is a part of the appraisal process. Are property values increasing, stable, or declining? What is the overall supply and demand of the market? Is there a housing shortage of a particular type of home (3BR, 2BA ranch for example)? Is the market in balance or in over supply? How long has the house been on the market? What are the mean/median sales prices, number of homes for sale, number of pending sales, number of closed sales, days on the market, months supply, price per sq ft.?

Here are some things a real estate appraiser will analyze as part of the appraisal process:

Property Characteristics

- **Location:** The neighborhood, proximity to community amenities, schools, shopping, restaurants, recreational activities, employment, and overall desirability.

- **Size:** Square footage of the property, lot size, and the number of bedrooms and bathrooms.

- **Condition:** The age of the property, updates or renovations, and overall condition.

- **Features:** Special features such as a pool, garage, fireplace, landscaping, functional utility, heating/cooling, energy efficiency items, porch/deck/patio/sunroom, or other amenities/upgrades.

- **Views:** Positive views that are desirable for the market including water, golf course, or other desirable privacy views. Negative views could include a busy road or other undesirable views.

- **Quality:** Building material and workmanship of exterior and interior of dwelling such as brick vs. vinyl exterior; tile flooring vs laminate vinyl; granite countertops vs. formica; and custom vs spec homes.

- **Design:** Style and design of homes attract different markets. A one story home most likely will attract an older demographic while a 2 story home will most likely attract a younger aged market with families.

- **Age:** Actual age is the number of years that have passed since construction was completed (year built). Effective age is an estimate of how old the house appears to be based on current condition and maintenance.

Comparable Properties (Comps):

- **Recently Sold Properties:** Analyzing properties similar to the subject property. Appraisers search within one year of the effective date. Most recent sales are best, ideally the past 3-6 months. In an increasing/declining market comps should be within 3 months.

- **Active Listings:** Properties that are currently on the market. While these don't show the final sale price, they give insight into what sellers are currently asking for similar properties.

- **Pending Listings:** Properties that are under contract but not yet closed. These can indicate what buyers are willing to pay in the current market.

- **Expired/Withdrawn Listings:** Properties that were listed but did not sell, which may indicate an unrealistic asking price or other issues.

Market Conditions:

- **Supply and Demand:** The balance between the number of properties for sale and the number of buyers in the market.

- **Market Trends:** Understanding whether the market is trending upwards, downwards, or staying flat, based on recent sales data and economic indicators.

- **Seasonality:** Real estate markets can fluctuate based on the time of year, with certain seasons seeing more activity than others.

Adjustments:

- **Price Adjustments:** Adjustments are made to the comps to account for differences in size, condition, location, and features. This ensures that the comparisons are as accurate as possible.

- **Time Adjustments:** Adjustments for the time elapsed since the contract date (considered the "meeting of the minds" between the parties) of a comparable property, especially in increasing or declining markets.

CHAPTER 4:

Preparing for a Property Appraisal

(✗) MYTH	(✓) REALITY
Homeowners should always make major renovations before an appraisal.	Not all renovations add value, and some may not yield a return on investment. Appraisers focus on market-relevant improvements.

If you have made changes to your home, now's the time to highlight any improvements, upgrades, repairs, and renovations. Help your home appraiser know everything about your property that could add value. See chapter 8 for more about what renovations and upgrades add the most value.

Documentation to Provide

- Upgrades/renovations/ additions to property and approximate year (and approximate cost if appropriate and available) including kitchen/baths

- Mechanical, electrical, and plumbing systems

- Water heater

- Roof

- Exterior siding

- Windows

- Floor coverings

- Updated surveys

- Any other information the homeowner or real estate agent thinks would help the appraiser accurately value the home.

- Comps can be provided but it is up to the appraiser whether or not to use them in the report.

Cleaning and Maintenance Tips

A well-maintained house is easier to sell and more attractive to buy. Address problems before they get too big and too expensive to fix. Keep the house updated in line with the market if you're planning to sell. Keep exterior landscaping groomed. Keep the house sound, safe, and secure. A well-maintained house will help keep the effective age low, meaning less depreciation in the appraisal.

Examples: securing handrails on porches, eliminating tripping hazards; updating wiring/ electrical hazards; eliminating water intrusions; add carbon monoxide detectors, especially if you have an attached garage, fireplace, gas stove, or other combustible material.

These items don't necessarily increase/decrease value much but they indicate how the house is maintained (poorly or well maintained). FHA and some lenders require a sound, safe, and secure dwelling including the above items.

Deferred maintenance should be addressed including rotten siding, missing siding, missing roofing, or anything that will allow water, rodents, insects, wood-destroying insects, or animals to intrude and cause damage to the dwelling.

A real estate appraiser does not include or note personal property in reports. However, if it is a purchase/transfer, the home appraiser shall note any personal (non-realty) transfers to the buyer at no value. No personal property is to be considered in the report.

CHAPTER 5:

Common Home Appraisal Methods

 MYTH

Appraisers always use comparable sales (comps) from within the past six months.

 REALITY

While recent comps are ideal, appraisers may use older data if necessary, especially in unique markets or when there are fewer recent sales.

Comps are what most people think are the number one driver of a home's appraised value. Comparable sales and price per square foot are pieces of the equation, but lots of factors determine the bottom line value. Pour another cup of coffee friends, we're about to get into numbers and formulas! Don't worry, I got you.

Price Per Square Foot

It's important to note that price per square foot isn't always the best way to determine a property's value. Think of it this way: you might have two cars with similar interior space, but they could be completely different when it comes to features, quality, and condition. So, pricing a car based on cubic footage wouldn't make much sense—just like price per square foot doesn't tell the whole story when valuing a home.

The interior cubic footage of these two cars may be similar but they are completely different cars in terms of amenities, quality, condition, etc. Therefore, price per cubic foot would not be the best way to determine the value of a car.

Value is determined by the adjusted sales price of the comps.

Sales comparison is considered the most appropriate indicator of market value.

Comps = Comparable Sales Approach

When using the sales comparison approach, it's important to look at sales from the past year that are similar to the subject property. This means finding comparable homes in terms of location, lot size, view, design, quality, age, condition, square footage, and the number of bedrooms and bathrooms. Other things to consider are whether the homes have garages or carports, outdoor spaces like porches and patios, upgrades and amenities, fireplaces, sheds, fences, pools, and any other permanent improvements.

For location, the appraiser should search the neighborhood first, then the market for comparable criteria. Design-wise, it's important to compare homes with similar layouts—one-story homes are part of a different market than two-story homes, so try to find comps that match. You also want to focus on similar exterior finishes (like brick versus vinyl) and quality levels (from Q1 to Q6). Condition matters too, so you'll be looking at homes in similar states (rated from C1 to C6). For square footage, the appraiser looks for comps that are within approximately 20% of the heated living area of the subject property. Bedroom and bathroom count also play a role—a one-bedroom home is quite different from a two- or three-bedroom, but the gap between four and five bedrooms isn't as significant.

Location: 1 mile radius for urban; 2 mile radius for suburban; 5 mile radius for rural.

Design: 1 story vs 2 stories (two different markets) so try to use comps similar in story.

Quality: similar exterior finishes (brick vs vinyl). Q1, Q2, Q3, Q4, Q5, Q6

Condition: C1, C2, C3, C4, C5, C6

Heated Square Footage: : approximately +/- 20%

BR/BA: 1br vs 2br vs 3br is much different. However, 4br vs 5br there is not as much difference.

In residential real estate appraisals, quality levels (Q1 through Q6) are used to describe the overall construction quality of a home, from the highest to the lowest. Here's a breakdown:

- **Q1: Exceptional Quality –** Custom-built homes with unique, high-end materials and craftsmanship. Everything is top-of-the-line, from finishes to structural details.

- **Q2: High Quality –** Similar to Q1 but slightly less extravagant. High-quality materials and finishes, often found in custom or semi-custom homes.

- **Q3: Above Average Quality –** Well-built homes with good materials and finishes. These are typically found in well-maintained suburban neighborhoods.

- **Q4: Average Quality –** Standard construction with average-grade materials. Common in most residential homes, like those in typical subdivisions.

- **Q5: Below Average Quality** – Basic construction with lower-cost materials. These homes are functional but lack significant upgrades or high-end finishes.

- **Q6: Substandard Quality** – Homes built with minimal attention to detail and the cheapest materials. These may be poorly constructed or in poor condition.

The physical condition of the home is rated one through six, from best to worst. Here's a breakdown:

- **C1: Excellent Condition** – Recently built or with recently constructed improvements and has not been previously occupied. The entire structure and all components are new and the dwelling features no physical depreciation.

- **C2: Very Good Condition** – Slightly older than C1 but still very well-maintained. Minimal signs of wear, with recent upgrades or renovations.

- **C3: Good Condition** – Average wear and tear for the home's age. Well-maintained, but some minor repairs or updates may be needed.

- **C4: Average Condition** – Normal wear and tear for its age, with some maintenance issues. Some components may need updating or repair, but the home is fully functional.

- **C5: Fair Condition** – Noticeable deferred maintenance. Several repairs are needed, and some systems or components may be nearing the end of their life.

- **C6: Poor Condition** – Significant issues with deferred maintenance and potentially structural problems. The home may not be fully functional and needs major repairs.

Typically, the most weight is placed on the first three comps, and you can assign different percentages to them based on their relevance.

Adjustments

Value Adjustments
Sales or Financing Concessions
Date of Sale/Time
Location
Leasehold/Fee Simple
Site
View
Design (Style)
Quality of Construction
Actual Age
Condition
Above Grade Room Count Gross Living Area
Basement & Finished Rooms Below Grade
Functional Utility
Heating/Cooling
Energy Efficient Items
Garage/Carport
Porch/Patio/Deck
Amenities/Upgrades
Fireplace
Other
Net Adjustment (Total)
Adjusted Sale Price of Comparables

A real estate appraiser will input the comps into a grid (like excel spreadsheet) and compare each line item (subject vs comp), then make adjustments on each line item in the grid.

When it comes to making adjustments, appraisers use several methods, like paired sales analysis, regression analysis, or depreciated cost of improvements, to back up the adjustments. Once all the adjustments are made, you'll see the adjusted sales price listed at the bottom for each comparable property (or "comp"). The value of the home being appraised will typically fall somewhere within the range of these adjusted sales prices.

If adjustments exceed 10% on one line item they need to be explained. For example, a comp property extends past the boundaries of the search parameter guidelines, that needs to be explained. If a comp property is superior in one feature, lenders like to see another comp that's inferior in that same feature. Across the board adjustments must be explained and well-supported.

What is a Regression Analysis?

Regression analysis in residential real estate appraisals is a statistical method used to figure out how different property features impact its value. By analyzing sales data from a large number of homes, this method helps appraisers understand the relationship between certain variables—like square footage, lot size, or number of bedrooms—and the sales price.

Home appraisers use regression analysis to make more accurate adjustments when comparing properties. This approach is especially helpful when it's tough to find exact comps that match the subject property.

It's important because it brings an extra layer of precision to the appraisal process. Instead of just relying on a handful of similar properties, regression analysis leverages a wider data set to ensure adjustments are based on actual market behavior, making the final value more reliable.

What is Paired Sales Analysis?

Paired sales analysis in residential real estate appraisals is a method where two very similar homes are compared, with the main difference being one specific feature, like a garage or a renovated kitchen. By looking at how much more (or less) one home sold for compared to the other, appraisers can figure out the value of that particular feature. Unlike regression analysis, which uses a large set of data and statistical methods, paired sales analysis looks at individual sales to make direct comparisons. This method is often used when there are only a few comparable properties and it's important because it gives appraisers a clear, side-by-side view of how certain features impact home values.

Home appraisers rank the comps—1st, 2nd, 3rd, and so on—based on how similar they are to the property. Usually, the top three comps are the most relevant. From there, the appraiser decides which comps carry the most weight in the final decision. They can emphasize one comp more than the others or spread the weight across all of them. In the end, the appraiser's final opinion of value is shaped by this process, and sometimes they'll even assign specific percentages to the comps in the final value reconciliation.

Cost Approach

The Cost Approach in home appraisals is mainly used when a property is new or unique, and there aren't enough comparable sales to rely on. It estimates value by figuring out how much it would cost to build the home from scratch, then subtracts any depreciation (wear and tear). Unlike the Sales Comparison Approach, which looks at recent sales of similar homes, the Cost Approach focuses more on

Opinion of site value

Dwelling sf x $/SF

Por/ptio/SP, etc. lump sum cost

Garage/carport sq ft x $/sf

Total estimate cost-new

Less physical/functional/external depreciation. age/life method: eff age/lifespan = depreciation

Depreciated cost of improvements

Site improvements

= total cost

the actual costs of construction and land value. This method is particularly useful for appraising custom homes or properties with few comps. Most lenders require this approach on new construction.

Most lenders require appraisers to utilize a national standard like the Marshall & Swift Estimator.

Income Approach for Investment Properties

The Income Approach to residential real estate appraisals is used for properties that are primarily investments, like rental homes or multi-family units. It values the property based on the monthly market rent that are rented on a monthly basis (not short term rentals) by estimating the monthy rental income and expenses, then

Comparable rentals adjusted rental price.

Estimated monthly market rent x GRM (gross rent multiplier) = value by income approach

GRM is determined by comparable sales price/comp rent price.

Ex: $250,000 (SP) / $1700 (rent price) = 147 grm

calculating its value as an investment. This differs from the Cost Approach, which focuses on what it would cost to rebuild the home, and the Sales Comparison Approach, which looks at recent sales of similar properties. The Income Approach is most helpful when the property's earning potential is the main factor in determining its value.

CHAPTER 6:

How to Read A Home Appraisal Report

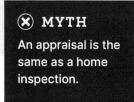

MYTH

An appraisal is the same as a home inspection.

REALITY

Appraisals assess the overall value, while inspections focus on the property's condition and potential issues.

Don't expect your appraisal to note any failures of systems, things that need to be replaced or repaired, previous water damage, encroaching lot lines on a neighboring property, and code violations. Those types of issues (and many more!) are found in an inspection report, which we recommend you get when buying a property.

What *can* you expect in your appraisal report and what does it all mean?

How to Read the Appraisal Value

Typically on the bottom of page 2 under comps 1, 2, and 3, there is the value by sales comparison, cost approach, and income approach. The final opinion is the bottom number as of a certain date (effective date).

Common Terminology and Metrics

- **Assignment Types:** Types of property assignments like purchase, refinance, or new construction.

- **Transaction Types:** REO sale; short sale; court ordered sale; estate sale; relocation sale; non-arms length sale; arms length sale.

- **Urban/Suburban/Rural:** Categories describing the property's location and density of development. Urban is typically built up over 75%, higher population area, and is closer to the central business district (CBD). A Suburb is typically built up 25-75% and is the outskirts of the city/town or smaller community adjacent to a city/town. Rural is built up less than 25% with less population and no public services.

- **Demand/Supply:** The balance of buyer demand versus available properties in the market. High demand w/ low supply the prices increase. Low demand w/ high supply prices will decrease.

- **Marketing Time:** How long a property typically takes to sell under current market conditions. In appraisal terms, marketing time is categorized either: -under 3 months; 3-6 months; or over 6 months.

- **General Description of the Property:** An overview of the property's size, style, and use. Also includes existing/proposed/under construction; year built; and age.

- **Foundations:** The type of foundation the property is built on (e.g., slab, crawlspace, pilings, basement-type and size of basement).

- **Exterior/Interior Descriptions:** Details about the materials and condition of the property's outside and inside. Including foundation walls; exterior walls; roof surface; gutters/downspouts; window type; storm sash/insulated/non-insulated; screens.

- **Improvements:** Anything permanently attached to a property. Examples include a dwelling, car storage, porch/patio/decks, in ground pool, fence.

- **Condition and Quality Ratings:** Standard ratings (e.g., Q1-Q6, C1-C6) that assess the property's build quality and condition.

- **Conformity:** How well the property fits into its neighborhood in terms of design and use.

- **Adverse Conditions:** Negative factors affecting the property, like zoning issues or environmental hazards.

- **Transaction Types (Sales):** Specific sale types like arms-length, short sale, or court-ordered sales.

- **Financing Types:** Methods of financing a property, including conventional loans, FHA, VA, seller financed, USDA, or cash sales.

- **Regression Analysis/Paired Sales Analysis:** Methods used to determine adjustments by analyzing comparable property data.

- **Adjusted Sales Price:** The final adjusted sales price of a comparable property after adjustments are made for differences compared to the subject.

CHAPTER 7:

Post Appraisal Steps

 MYTH
An appraisal is the final word on a property's value and cannot be challenged.

 REALITY
Appraisals can be disputed or reviewed, especially if there are discrepancies or factual errors in the report.

A residential real estate appraisal is not the final word on the value of a home. While it provides a professional and well-researched estimate of a property's value based on market data and property features, it's still just one opinion. Market conditions, buyer interest, and negotiations can all influence the actual sale price. **Ultimately, the true value of a home is determined by what a buyer is willing to pay and what a seller is willing to accept.**

Addressing Discrepancies or Low Appraisals

Homeowners have the right to request a reconsideration of value (ROV) with the lender. Lenders have certain requirements. Examples include: suggested comps that should be more comparable than the comps utilized in the report (more recent sale, closer proximity, and more similar in terms of adjustments); adjustments that are not supported or explained. When requesting a reconsideration of value to the lender it is never acceptable to communicate a specific desired value or a minimum required value. **The reconsideration should focus on facts rather than opinions of specific value expectations. Avoid inappropriate or coercive language.**

Appealing an Appraisal

Homeowners can challenge an appraisal but unless you're the one who hired the appraiser, don't call the appraiser. Call and discuss your concerns with the lender, and the lender will discuss them with the appraiser. Reconsideration should include support for another opinion of value, not just because you think the value is wrong. Everybody has different opinions, but all opinions of value have to be supported with facts and data.

Errors and Omissions Policy (E&O)

An Errors and Omissions (E&O) report in a residential real estate appraisal is part of an insurance policy that protects the real estate appraiser from claims of negligence or mistakes made during the appraisal process. If an error in the appraisal leads to financial harm for a client, like a lender or homeowner, the E&O insurance can cover the legal costs or damages. It protects both the home appraiser, by providing liability coverage, and the clients, by offering recourse if a significant mistake affects the accuracy of the appraisal.

CHAPTER 8:

How To Enhance Your Home's Value

 MYTH
The appraisal amount equals the property's contract price.

 REALITY
The appraisal may be higher or lower than the contract price, depending on market conditions and the home appraiser's analysis.

If you're planning to sell your home, it's best to make sure the house shows well and all maintenance issues are taken care of, including exterior siding/roofing, landscaping has been groomed (curb appeal), interior floor covering, and walls are addressed/painted with neutral colors.

What Upgrades & Repairs Yield the Most ROI?

Job one is keeping a house up to date and properly maintained.

While the market will determine the value more than remodels and upgrades, if you're planning to remodel or update your property, be sure to do your homework on the market and see what level of upgrades/remodels your comps are attaining.

Be careful of overspending because the cost does not equal value.

Typically kitchen/living areas and baths are first to consider.

These areas are the most expensive but could also yield the most return on your investment.

Don't overbuild or underbuild in the neighborhood. Stay in line with what your market/neighborhood is at in terms of square footage, lot size, bedroom and bathroom count, garage, etc. You don't want to own the 5,000 sq. ft. house in a neighborhood of 1200 sq. ft. starter homes.

Curb Appeal and Landscaping

First impressions do matter! Curb appeal and landscaping show that you take care of the property and are important in attracting showings and standing out among other listings. However, landscaping typically does not return a good investment to increase value, so spend accordingly.

Energy Efficiency Improvements

Some of the energy efficiency improvements including air sealing, duct sealing, and proper insulation are the best returns on investment; however, they may not increase value. These items will help your energy bills and may be appealing to the homeowner or next buyer when they look at the cost of running the home. Other energy-efficiency items include solar panels, geo-thermal HVAC, energy-efficient windows, smart thermostats, tankless water heaters, attic ventilation, LED light bulbs, and appliance upgrades. However, do your homework to see if any comps have similar energy-efficient upgrades. If there are no comps that have done similar upgrades, then these upgrades are not likely to increase the value of your home.

Staging Your Home

You want your prospective buyers to see themselves living there. Decluttering and staging your home is a good, inexpensive way to create a vision in the mind of the buyer. If the market is hot and homes are selling quickly, it may not be necessary to stage a home. Your real estate agent can help you decide whether the cost is worth it.

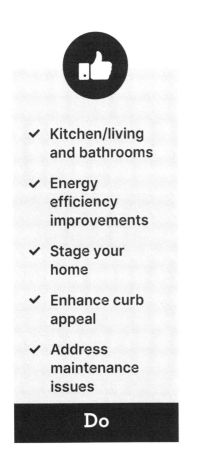

- ✔ Kitchen/living and bathrooms
- ✔ Energy efficiency improvements
- ✔ Stage your home
- ✔ Enhance curb appeal
- ✔ Address maintenance issues

Do

- ✖ Overspend
- ✖ Overbuild
- ✖ Forget curb appeal
- ✖ Forget to research market

Don't

CHAPTER 9:

Working with Real Estate Appraisers

MYTH

Appraisers only work for mortgage lenders.

REALITY

Appraisers can be hired by homeowners, investors, attorneys, or even government agencies for various purposes, including buying/selling, estate planning, divorce settlements, and tax disputes.

How Do You Find a Qualified Real Estate Appraiser?

If you're buying a home with a real estate agent and you need a mortgage loan, the lender will be the one hiring the home appraiser. If you're a homeowner seeking a pre-sale appraisal to assess the market value of your home or you're selling your home yourself, you will hire the appraiser. Real estate appraisers are independent and unbiased, working to provide an objective value estimate, regardless of who paid for the appraisal.

To find a qualified real estate appraiser, go to your state's appraisal board website.

In North Carolina: https://www.ncappraisalboard.org/

Search "real estate appraisers for (insert the city the home is in)". Property appraisers must be geographically competent. Search their online presence and website. Do they feel reputable? How long have they been in business? Do they have customer testimonials? Do they do the type of appraisal you need? Does their expertise meet your needs? Search their Google Business profile, do they have customer reviews? Search the Better Business Bureau for complaints against them.

Communicating Effectively with Your Home Appraiser

If the purpose of the report is for lending and the lender has ordered the appraisal, then the lender is the only one who can ask the appraiser to make changes to the report. Do not ask the appraiser to change the report unless you are the client. The home appraiser can receive requests only from clients.

Legal and Ethical Considerations

Make sure you are hiring a reputable, certified real estate appraiser who follows industry standards. A licensed appraiser can perform appraisals for the general public, however, only a certified appraiser is qualified to perform appraisals for lending institutions.

USPAP Compliance

- Uniform Standards of Professional Appraisal Practice (USPAP) promotes and maintains high public trust by establishing strict requirements.

- Confirm the report was developed and prepared in conformity with USPAP.

Report Accuracy

- Reports must be true, supported, credible, unbiased, and non-discriminatory.

- Analysis, opinions, and conclusions reflect the home appraiser's impartial, professional judgment.

Independence and Disclosure

- The home appraiser has no present or prospective interest in the property or parties involved.

- Disclosure is required if services were performed by this specific real estate appraiser on the property within the last 3 years.

- Engagement is not based on predetermined results.

- Compensation is not contingent on value favoring the client.

Ethical Obligations

- Disclose any person who provided significant assistance in developing the report.

- No bias, dishonesty, or discrimination in reporting.

- Home appraisers must accurately disclose observations and perform due diligence, including driving by comparables.

See https://www.appraisalfoundation.org/imis for more information.

CHAPTER 10:

FAQs and Expert Advice

1. What is a residential real estate appraisal?

An appraisal is an unbiased, professional estimate of a property's market value based on its current condition, location, and recent sales of comparable properties.

2. Why do I need a real estate appraisal?

Appraisals are typically required for mortgage loans, refinancing, tax assessments, divorce settlements, estate planning, or before selling or buying a property to determine its fair market value.

3. How long does an appraisal take?

The physical inspection usually takes from 10-45 minutes, depending on the property's size and complexity. The entire process, including research and report preparation, typically takes several days to a week.

4. What factors do appraisers consider when valuing a home?

Real estate appraisers consider the property's location, size, condition, floor plan, amenities, and comparable sales in the area. They also assess market trends, neighborhood characteristics, and any improvements or upgrades.

5. What is the difference between an appraisal and a home inspection?

An appraisal estimates the market value of a property, focusing on its general characteristics and comparable sales. A home inspection is a detailed evaluation of the property's condition, identifying any issues or repairs needed.

During the Appraisal Process

6. Can I choose my home appraiser?

Typically, the lender selects the appraiser to ensure objectivity. However, you can hire your own appraiser for independent purposes, such as pre-listing or dispute resolution.

7. Should I be present during the appraisal?

You can be present, but it's not required. Being there allows you to answer any questions the home appraiser might have about the property or provide information on recent upgrades.

8. What should I do to prepare for an appraisal?

Ensure the property is clean and accessible, provide a list of recent upgrades or renovations, and have any necessary documents ready, such as any change in the property's survey or recent change in ownership that may not be recorded by public record.

After the Appraisal

9. What happens if the home's appraisal comes in lower than the purchase price?

If the appraisal is lower than the agreed-upon contract price, the buyer and seller may need to renegotiate the price, the buyer may need to bring more money to the table, or the deal could fall through if a compromise isn't reached.

10. Can I challenge or appeal the appraisal value?

Yes, if you believe the appraisal is not credible, you can provide additional information or comparable sales data to the lender or appraiser and request a reconsideration.

11. How long is an appraisal valid?

An appraisal is valid for one day (effective date); however, typically they are considered current within 3 months of the effective date, unless there have been any recent good comparable sales.

12. Will renovations or upgrades increase my appraisal value?

Renovations can increase your appraisal value, especially if they align with market trends and are in areas like kitchens, bathrooms, or energy efficiency. However, not all improvements will provide a high return on investment.

13. What if my home has unique features?

If your home has unique features that aren't common in your area, the appraiser will make adjustments based on similar properties or other factors that contribute to market value.

Specific Situations

14. Do residential real estate appraisers consider foreclosures or short sales in their assessment?

The appraiser will consider all sales and typically will use sales that have similar terms as the subject (foreclosures, short sale, etc.). If foreclosures and short sales are common in the market then they should be considered and used in the report as a comparable sale.

15. Can I use the same appraisal for different lenders?

Some lenders may accept a recent appraisal if it meets their guidelines, but others may require a new one. It's best to check with the specific lender.

CONCLUSION

Thank you for exploring the *Pocket Guide to Residential Real Estate Appraisals in North Carolina*. I hope this guide has provided you with valuable insights into the world of real estate appraisals, from understanding what an appraisal entails, to preparing for it, and interpreting the results.

In this guide, we've covered everything from the basics of appraisals and the appraisal process, to the factors influencing home value, and the different methods used in appraisals. We've also provided practical advice for preparing your home, understanding and using your appraisal report, and enhancing your home's value.

Whether you're a property buyer, seller, or real estate professional, this guide aims to demystify the home appraisal process, helping you make informed decisions and navigate the complexities with confidence. By addressing common myths and providing expert advice, I hope to empower you to take control of your real estate journey and achieve the best possible outcomes.

Thank you for allowing me to be part of your real estate experience. If you have any further questions or need additional guidance, feel free to reach out.

For more detailed information and expert insights,
visit www.ajcottleappraisers.com.

About the Author

Albert Jay Cottle III

Jay Cottle III was born and raised in Wilmington, NC and graduated in 1999 from East Carolina University with a degree in Construction Management and a minor in Business. He began his career in commercial construction with Clancy & Theys, contributing to major projects like the Fort Fisher Aquarium and UNCW classroom buildings. In 2006, he transitioned to residential construction, launching his own business.

After gaining certification in home energy efficiency audits and renovations, Jay returned to Wilmington to partner with his father as a residential real estate appraiser. With more than a decade of experience, he specializes in appraising new construction, purchases, refinances, and land across several North Carolina counties. When not working, Jay enjoys tennis, racquetball, and spending time with his wife Lara and daughter Mary-Myers.

Read Jay's informative blog and find additional real estate appraisal resources at ajcottleappraisers.com.

Made in the USA
Middletown, DE
06 February 2025